Cold Water Memory

poems

Greg Watson

Cold Water Memory

Second Edition
Copyright © 2021 Greg Watson
All rights reserved.

Originally published in 2001
by
March Street Press

Credits
Cover Photo: Pixabay courtesy of standuppaddle
Author Photo: Jordana Torgeson
Layout: Vida Raine

ISBN13: 9798598162538

Acknowledgements

"Night Work" appeared in
Ibettson St. Press

"I Trace the Lines of Every Poem" appeared in
Insomnia & Poetry

"Figure in the Rain," "Winter Poem," "Yes, It Is," and
"Rain in New Orleans" appeared in
Newsletter Inago

"In an Imaginary Barn Alone" appeared in
Thin Coyote and *South Ash Press*

"Museum" appeared in
Nerve Cowboy

"Moving" appeared in
Writer's Journal

"With Molly at the Bad Habit Cafe" appeared in
First Class

"Outside the Uptowner Cafe, Thinking of the Afternoon
She Did Not Die" appeared in
Thin Coyote

"First Snow" appeared in
Newsletter Inago and *Devil Blossoms*

"Hypothesis" appeared in
The Old Red Kimono

"November Feeling" appeared in
Understanding Magazine

"The Sculptor" and "Procession" appeared in
Sulphur River Literary Review

"The Bloodlines of Leaves" appeared in
Poetic Page, *Short Stories Bimonthly*, and *Poetic Eloquence*

Titles by Greg Watson

All the World at Once: New and Selected Poems

What Music Remains

The Distance Between Two Hands

Things You Will Never See Again

Pale Light from a Distant Room

Cold Water Memory

Annmarie Revisions

Open Door, Open Wall

Many titles available from Amazon and Nodin Press

www.amazon.com

www.NodinPress.com

Other Contributions

The Road by Heart: Poems of Fatherhood

Edited by Greg Watson and Richard Broderick

published by Nodin Press

CONTENTS

*"In the midst of winter,
I finally learned there was, in me,
an invincible summer."*

— Albert Camus

WE THINK WE KNOW THE WORLD

We think we know the world,
that which offers itself to plain sight,
cupped in outstretched palms;
but at night it is daylight
that is the imposter,
and we who lack credentials.
The stars blink on and off,
the moon thinks perhaps you
look familiar, but has lost
both your name and address.

FIRST SNOW

It has come early this year,
dragging its bony silence through the streets
like the billowing ghost of Christ,
clothes heavy and white upon the line.
On every corner men and women
bend their backs in stoic determination,
talk of blizzards from decades past.
Cars stall, dogs step tentatively
upon the shifting ground.
Loose change echoes in newspaper stands,
the knife-sharp jangle of turning keys;
the streetlights speak in code.
Someone has sketched an alphabet
in the snow, and the name Sofia.
One continuous word
for the wind to simply blow away.

NOCTURNE

It is a quiet night, rain dribbling
down the window glass
like words left unspoken,
words now finding their way
slowly back to the earth.
A family of sparrows shelters
below the roof's awning,
driving the cats mad with instinct
they do and do not understand.

Is it not you that I miss but
the idea of who we once were,
such quiet understanding
driven away by anger,
suspicion, the small and pointless
cruelties of youth?
Is memory merely the clothing
we wear when we become
suddenly too old to lie?

Outside, the traffic has died
to barely a whisper,
the rumor of movement
and nothing more.
Shadows layer upon shadows,
cross the walls like leaden boats
carrying great rooms

of starlight that we are not
yet allowed to see.

The way I sleep now is
the way I will refuse
when the real sleep comes.

HOLLOW

There's a hole in my chest the size of a small nation, a hollow that opens into deepest autumn, wind blowing through like cold water, a thousand needle pricks in the hand that carries this heart to rest. Torn pages of leaves tumble through, sprinkling their dust, colors dripping like the dye of an old lover's dress. So many houses and faces I pass unnoticed, an ordinary man walking wounded with his thoughts, folds of light and reason bundling up for the coming cold. The gray-bone cold of rain on barbed wire, the cold if you were made of body alone, or simply alive enough to consider it.

HYPOTHESIS

Perhaps the compulsion
to write poems
comes not from the gods
but from their absence,
from the open sheets
of sky they leave us
on which we scribble our
hasty messages home.

WITH MOLLY AT THE BAD HABIT CAFE

We smell of winter, the cold clinging to sweaters,
scarves, and breath; sip foam from black lacquered mugs
large enough to cup in both hands, an oversized book of
ancient catacombs stretched between us. Passing cars
cast net-like shadows across the walls, a death-rattle
blues rising through the steam, clang, and clatter of
espresso machines. With one slender hand she extracts a
short filterless cigarette from a narrow silver case. Her
hair, a tiger's nest of red, a faint halo of dye along her
hairline, her leather jacket worn and greenish at creases
and elbows. Outside, men and women totter past in
layers of down and wool, heads lowered against the
wind. The city is frozen in body and in time. I want to
stay here at this cafe, the puddles beneath our boots
unmoving for hours. I want to stay here and watch this
woman smoke.

RAIN MUSIC

This night, too cold for crickets or spirits past, rain so silent the grass is unsure. A violin on the radio is weeping. It is the music of stoic-minded stars turning toward reflection, the window glass beginning to breathe. It is a thousand magnetic spiders stretching silk into light and light into sound. It is all sound and all sorrow in linear transition, from empty box to broken bottle, this endless distillation of unused tears.

Such alchemy cannot last. Soon it will all fall like furniture, like men, this city of light buried beneath the endless clamor of armor. I turn the volume down, turn back to the poem I was writing before writing this. I prefer the sound of a single soul. I prefer the weeping.

PROCESSION

The autumn leaves grow brittle, curled
and clinging in the chill-damp air; old men
in coal-colored suits shuffle and smoke, buttonholes
blooming the gold of forgotten suns.

The long procession of automobiles,
cold and lacquered as museum pieces, crawls
grudgingly along the blacktop,
small, nationless flags waving from each.

A woman the age and pallor of the sidewalk
watches, arms folded against the wind,
mouths a name in silence
waiting for the light to change.

I TRACE THE LINES OF
EVERY POEM

I trace the lines of every poem
I have not yet written,
here along the contours of your body
languid in the lamplight
as I read, a slight and spidery
braille you are too weary tonight
to translate or instruct.

DO THE GODS MISS US?

Do the gods miss us when we don't write?
Do the trees miss our clumsy descriptions?
Do I remember my way through
the simplest of days, when language recedes,
trailing off like steps quietly erased
in an overnight snowfall?
Words flutter from the page
like moths, shake off their ink,
play dead. I am not amused.
I kick at them, those black wooden engines,
move my flat-tipped fingers from
side to side, as if conducting an orchestra
while the notes have all agreed
to return to their source.
Is this then the fate for one unable
to sit in a room without naming,
without calling attention to those things
better left alone, those things trying
to teach you something outside of *want*?
I dress, I shave, dreaming of new
superstitions, new ways of mourning.
This day has no need of a name,
though the silence you hear is a silence
with a story to tell.

WINTER POEM

In deep winter, the bones of the highway
crack beneath its frozen weight.
Long stretches of roads fill with ghosts,
casting thin, uncertain shadows.
Night bleeds into day like water into stone;
beer cans glint in swollen banks
of snow, proud as soldiers in formation.
In the distance, bare-knuckled trees
stretch like fractures in the empty sky,
the gated refineries crackle and
smoke to keep us alive.
Now is the time to drink whiskey,
read the classics, reassess,
let whiskers grow white.
Now the poets brood like professionals,
cursing the cold pinpricks of wind,
the moon hardened like a frozen pond.
But the poet knows next to nothing:
for months he pines and prays for spring,
and is soon complaining
of the mud on his underused boots.

MOVING

Near the first of the month, especially these
waning days of summer, the same ritual begins.
The moving vans arrive, ready to receive
the accumulation of our daily lives:
stacks of brown boxes labeled kitchen
or bedroom, tall black trashcan liners
bulging and shifting with odd animal-like shapes.
Box springs and mattresses — some with coils
shot through, some stained with sweat,
still bearing the shape of bodies turning —
sail from the tops of automobiles.
Socks and undergarments leap from
warped dresser drawers; a bright floral
sunhat breezes down the sidewalk
tumbling and spinning in yellows and reds.
College students emerge with their wiry
floor lamps and fiber board desks,
leaving clear plastic crates and card tables,
stacks of textbooks lining the curb
with a sign marked, "Free. Please take."
They are in a great hurry, it seems,
darting this way and that, anxious to keep
moving, anxious to begin again.
Even when backing up the U-Haul,
its single note signaling over and over,
they hardly bother to look behind.

FIGURE IN THE RAIN

In quiet repose you hold the doorway
upright, smoking as if smoking
were an act of God, breathless glow
of downcast face amid
streams of cinder-black hair;
wind-strewn shadows stretched
the very length of desire,
impossible spark of blood and stone
struck from the match
that smolders at your feet.

Woman among women, beautiful damage,
painter of broken wings,
now could I stand
bloodstream to bloodstream
with you and never want
for water again.

CEREMONY

Outside the bus shelter a young woman,
dressed in an army surplus jacket,
blue skirt with yellow fringes,
reads a book of Spanish poems.
She thumbs the pages front to back,
then back again, her dark hair
falling across one eye.
Then, one by one, she begins
setting the corners of each page
on fire, thumbing her disposable
lighter the way someone else
might thumb the beads of a rosary.
The ashes scatter like crow dust,
funeral confetti for a dirge,
a mourning only she can hear.
I know neither her name
nor her story, but believe in
her song completely.
She calls forth the saints by name,
and knows this wind by heart.

I HEAR THE WOMEN OF SUMMER

I hear the women of summer weeping, there in the heat-saturated street where the cat has been suddenly thrown, the car of one woman stopped but a second too late. In a moment they have become the only two people in the world, sobbing, pacing, speaking emphatically into outstretched palms. The sun burns down, the breeze lifts the green leaves in small, hesitant waves. Everything slows, everything blurs at the edges. I want to hold these women, to offer up some secret wisdom that I simply do not possess. I watch their shadows, fixed upon the sidewalk, reluctant, it seems, to follow their forms. We are strangers here, knowing only that our time is so brief, and these days of summer so very, very long.

OUTSIDE THE UPTOWNER CAFE, THINKING OF THE AFTERNOON SHE DID NOT DIE

Well, we go on; one hand floating weightless as a balloon, the body pulling itself down again. Our bones can only be lifted so much, and the ocean is so vast before us. Though a residue remains, like nicotine on the fingers or a thumbprint on the soul, and it belongs the way a bruise belongs, the way our shadows smolder when shut away for the night.

Today I walk with neither haste nor direction, the sex and the sorrow of sad letter days discarded, the fact of my age, name, and profession lost to the angular wind. I carry your words in one pocket, your silence in the other. The soft glow of your childlike face gazes back at me and back upon itself, foreign postage on a postcard never sent. How can I answer now, knowing this business of words, this stooge's religion, to be merely diversion? We go on, each in our way. Our bones can only be lifted so much. But the body is such a stubborn guest. We may as well set the table.

RAIN IN NEW ORLEANS

All day it came down like bullets, so heavy
and so fast it seemed an imitation
of rain. Gray taxis stalled

in the narrow streets, buildings and people
suddenly far away, grainy as
ancient tintypes. The museums

swelled and the music slowed to a waltz.
Tourists rushed by in bright summer clothes,
one-page concert programs creased

and creased again like overstuffed match-
books, their dime store umbrellas
collapsing like broken corsets.

Brass bands huddled together like criminals
under wind-frayed awnings, and tap boys
danced shirtless on every corner,

sinewy as copperheads, solid as railroad iron,
so frantic, so furious that neither wind
nor rain could touch them.

NOVEMBER FEELING

There's a candle in the window,
there where you once
lived, signaling its place
in the air over and over again.
The moon burns like a
blister on the rough hand of night,
a night so dark that shadows
seem strangely illuminated
and no one dares to walk alone,
not even the rain.
From the roads below,
just out of view, a final warmth
of wind, thin, sputtering,
rising with the distant hiss
of ocean, a muscle of water
once strong enough to
spit out ships as afterthought.
Withered leaves circle
toward the earth in patterns
of their own design;
trees and men grown longer
than memory, craning
their necks to listen.

A FURTHER LOGIC

There is no scientific evidence
in support of palmistry,
or the scattered wisdom of coffee grounds,
nor tin cast for the new year.

Yet should I take and marry your eyes,
or give up food and lodging
for the warmth of your womanhood,
who could dispute my reasoning?

SLUMP

I haven't had a new thought
in a long, long while.

No wonder you keep
getting in.

CONFLICT

A man who has trouble speaking
will sit for hours before a machine,
typing out his innate defiance
against the failure of his voice.
Without his hands he cannot speak.
Yet there is caution even in this:
to insist upon one word is to
admit the possibility of another,
to know also the silence
that surrounds it.

THE SCULPTOR

When she sees a bicycle, standing skeletal in the snow, she sees also the dragon's sharpened wings, the dagger glinting in a dram of water, the blooming asphodel that scissors could not kill. A thousand ancient mariners dangle from her window, wondering at the sound of her voice, how she could know them, their drowning and return. She grants them a baptism of blowtorch and saw, hauls them up into the light. Sculpture records. Sculpture remembers where history forgets. When she leaves this place, it is as if from one world to another, walking this pallid city in plain disguise, weighing the reality of bread, wine, and clothing against the pleasures of the magpie. Tired of walking, she sleeps in her studio, surrounded by the cosmos of her design; the moon now copper-plated, sharp to the touch, the ship-gray stars looking down. Water, like shadow, begins to stir.

CALICO

It's four in the morning, the television
receding to a soft blue haze an hour ago;
the city yawning through its alleys
the stale-sour breath of seasons past.

Brittle leaves the color of ancient papyrus
crawl the uneven curbs
in search of severed branches
to somehow drink and green themselves again.

Everyone is fattening their blood now,
in fear of the hollowness of winter bones,
in fear of a great silence that leaves
even the crickets mute.

The cats come and go, quick with intent,
white bellies low to the ground,
shaking off entire lifetimes
like pearls of imaginary water.

The night is filled
with the flavor of our longing.

THREE POEMS FOR SPIDERS

1.

I wonder how the spiders survive
these lifeless winter rooms.
On what do they feed?
With what do they warm themselves,
when I must turn the valves
of radiators, wait for the gurgle
and hiss of steam rising
from the other side of the world?

2.

So much of my life is spent
in solitude, following the steps
of these small, blonde bodies,
only the sticky threads of their former
homes left as evidence.
Finding them here, startled or
folded in silence, poorly camouflaged
between toilet seats, books,
window blinds, we acknowledge
our mutual strangeness,
the endless surprise of this life.

3.

Last night I dreamed of a dark spider
ticking in my wristwatch,
seemingly calm under glass,
legs shifting their tiny shadows
into seconds, minutes, entire days.
I woke with a fever, the world
still silent, and the sudden
taste of daylight on my tongue.

MONOLOGUE

Thinking back over
the years, I realize that
I was speaking only
to myself.

I may as well continue
doing so now.

THE FINAL IMAGE

The final image of your body
should be enough
for one life's blessing.

Why then this constant need
for revision?

THE BELLS

I wake to the sound of cathedral bells
outside the window, so distant
and so muffled it is as though they
were ringing from somewhere
deep within the earth.
For a moment, I can almost
smell them, that cold, damp smell
of iron filling the room, hovering
like breath around the body.
The crows don't seem to notice,
continuing their endless arguments,
every caw a curse or a warning.
It is early, the neighbors not
quite awake, dragging their clumsy
shoulders into doorframes,
rubbing eyes back into sight.
East of this city, a man dreams
of flying, of the cruciform his shadow
casts on the sidewalk below,
the buildings bathed in blue light.
And then the bells, the bells
that the world for now ignores.

MUSEUM

There are no doors here.
One walks through one wall
to the next.

COCKROACH POEM

I imagine the cockroaches from that first dingy
apartment, barely more than one windowless room, to be
alive and well, still scurrying at the sudden intrusion of
light, still surviving on crumbs, hair, or nothing,
seemingly, but air. Unlike us, their demands are few, their
concept of dignity based only on continuation. I
remember the crunch of their hardened bodies, smooth
and glinting like rainbows in the gasoline slicks of alleys.
I remember their sheer numbers, those distant cousins of
the hydra, old as dinosaurs yet continually new,
resurfacing from every shadow. I imagine them older
now, perhaps slower, toughened by endurance; their
offspring grown, ready to find an alarm clock radio or
cupboard of their own to move into. They will outlive
these lines as well, gnawing these pages until the sunlight
shines through, shining down upon their kingdom,
which shows no sign of waning, even now.

PHOTOGRAPH FOUND IN THE SLEEVE OF A 78

Duchin performs Gershwin, the radio dial of the hi-fi lit
like the skyline of a distant city. A stack of 78s is playing,
thick discs dropping one by one; between the notes a
faint crackling like rain heard through the thinnest of
walls. A slender young woman stands beside a small
window, her black taffeta dress unzipped near the neck,
where a lover's hand might rest. She wears medium
heels, silk stockings, small bright globes of earrings.
Perhaps she is waiting for someone now far away,
waiting for the stars to assemble and map the way home.
Look closely and you can see the Brooklyn Bridge, a blur
of fog-bound skyscrapers, as if they were somehow
walking away. In the narrow white border below, in a
script like small rolling waves, someone has written,
simply enough: "Lela, January 14, 1942."

NIGHT WORK

I dream awake in this old red chair,
drinking from darkened window glass,
winding time down with the mindless
persistence of a ghost or a saint.
The cats grow restless in these hours,
circling the amber-lacquered floors,
startled by the smallest shadow.
The noir movies roll past, landscapes
bathed in perpetual night, deceit.
The love poems seek only their subject,
as they have since time began.
The mind rumbles with hunger,
the heart wallows like a bullfrog
in arterial swamp. I cross the room,
the walls don't both to glance up,
gray-white emerging from gray-white,
the crumbling elegance of nothing.
The soul grows flabby between such walls,
a thing of lumps and quagmire.
We must learn to grow our flowers
here among the dung heaps,
to create words from unadorned air.
In the meantime, the walls stand,
the masters instruct only through silence.
I have written myself into a corner,
and hope to get out by daylight.

FROM THE VAULT

There are hidden floors in the mind
you can roll marbles across,
far alcoves you've never been before,
had never expected,
where a cold draft leads to a scent
and that scent to a slash of light.

Sometimes the mind itself is like sleeping
in a friendly stranger's house,
and sometimes that house
is haunted.

You walk around picking up old rags,
brittle fragments of paper
illegible yet somehow familiar,
wearing a jacket you thought you
had discarded years ago.

Cellars and attics swell to their ceilings
with artifice and artifact:
keys, shoes, letters, photographs,
walls bruised in yellows and blues,
weathered stone that answers
to your name.

Nothing is ever lost in these rooms.
Nothing lies still for long.

LINES WAITING FOR WINTER

A month of Sundays, and winter
coming on. There is no delaying it
now, no holding it back.

We begin each day with subtraction.
Only the shadows grow more
generous. Only their chill.

The clouds are dry and cracking,
the sky abandoned in haste.
Gravity tugs the sleeves of our coats.

We carry prayers in our pockets,
the taste of cathedral bells in back of
the throat. We ache, we slow.

A month of Sundays, and winter
coming on. There is no delaying it
now, no holding it back.

IN AN IMAGINARY BARN ALONE

A small girl, red as a freckle,
swallowing books like doorways,
catching cannonballs in her choking hair.

A single cross hangs unevenly,
its silence stretched for miles, bearing
the weight of a thousand mourners.

And the colors splashed across
the TV news, so beautiful you'd have
sworn she'd live forever.

POEM FOR HER THIRTY-FIRST YEAR

While you were away the house fell down.
The window glass reverted to wax
and the ceilings burned.
Three stray cats came to the stairwell,
comb-thin and mournful,
hungry for food and for touch,
to enter this most ordinary
kingdom as kings, crowned with
the heads of their kills.
A storm knocked the power out
for most of the day, a drab spectacle
for children and adults so long
removed from night.
I lit candles, squinted to read
Li Po, both of us reaching
for our separate moons.
Now you return, to sleep and dream,
undisturbed by it all, holding
this life as still as possible,
your leg reaching like a rudder
from the frame of the bed,
the precious metal of your earth-bound
hair, driven from salt mines
to mountains, where bells the size
of thumbnails ring out,
ring out for your safe return.

YES, IT IS

Is it necessary these lines be written?
Surely the earth will go on,
following its familiar course,
mindless as the wind,
welcoming rain, storm, and fire
in equal measure,
perhaps even better for
my silence.

Yet even if there is little to say
the pen moves involuntarily,
the typewriter hammers out its own
cause and record of the day.
Without this trail of words,
how can I navigate the simplest
beginning or ending,
how to acknowledge my own
steps, or hope to return?

I write to shake up the dust
the stars have thrown off, to walk
out into a world which merely
yawns in recognition.

WELLSPRING

Every breath
eventually returns
to the first,
and every love
to its source.

THE BLOODLINES OF LEAVES

The bloodlines of leaves map their way
through the palms of your hands,
words dripping like dream
upon the shoulders of the earth.

Perhaps the holiness is in the leaving,
the endless falling away
with little need for ceremony;
perhaps the wind itself
is a kind of psalm.

This is autumn. The summer birds
have flown, leaving their
bookmarks among the branches.
The highways too grow thin,
reticent in their shadows.

There is nothing here to fear
or to be taken away.
Sometimes a wound hurts
more when it is healing.

SUNLIGHT PIANO

Some day soon, or perhaps
many years from now,
on a night lost
to radio and satellite,
we will lie
side by side in a bed
softer than breath,
somewhere near the water
where the mosquitos
have grown slow
with sleepiness,
and I will turn to you
and you to me, and that
touch between us
will be like playing
a piano made of
sunlight in the middle
of a war, the worst,
last and greatest
history has yet thrown,
and we will go on
singing our little song
until we have
forgotten every word.

Greg Watson is the author of eight collections of poetry, most recently *All the World at Once: New and Selected Poems*. He is also co-editor with Richard Broderick of *The Road by Heart: Poems of Fatherhood*, published by Nodin Press.

Connect with Greg

Instagram
@gregwatsonpoet

Other Titles
available at

www.amazon.com
and
www.NodinPress.com